INTRODUCTION

The popularity of snakes as pets has been gaining momentum quite rapidly over the past few years. Many of the increasing numbers of dedicated people keeping and studying them have contributed to our knowledge of the technology required to keep these fascinating creatures in captivity, to ensure that they live long and healthy lives, and to breed them, preferably from generation to generation, so that the hobby can be supplied without damaging sometimes marginal wild populations.

This book has been produced for the benefit of anyone contemplating taking up the hobby of keeping the more popular varieties of snakes as pets and perhaps also breeding them. The following pages will provide you with all the facts required to do just that.

John Coborn
Nanango, Queensland, Australia

The striking beauty of many snakes, like this albino Ruthven's Kingsnake, *Lampropeltis ruthveni*, partially explains the rising popularity of snake-keeping.

Photo by Isabelle Francais

Photo by Isabelle Francais.

Many snake-keepers devote themselves to the large constrictors such as this green-phase Burmese Python, *Python molurus bivittatus*. These giants are not recommended for the beginning hobbist.

THE FASCINATION OF SNAKES

Ever since man walked the face of the earth, snakes have been an object of fear and fascination to him. Indeed, the snakes were already here before man evolved. The preoccupation of early man with serpents was perhaps not surprising. His closeness to nature meant that encounters

Today, we collectively know a lot more about snakes, though that does not stop a large part of the community from regarding them with a loathing unequaled to that directed at any other members of the animal kingdom with the possible exception of spiders. Even those infamous

More and more hobbyists are breeding their snakes, resulting in colors and patterns not normally seen in the wild. This "purple-blotched albino" Gopher Snake, *Pituophis catenifer*, is a good example.

Photo by W. P. Mara.

with snakes often would be part of his daily life. The fact that these lithe creatures could mysteriously move limblessly and rapidly over the ground must have given them an almost revered appeal. The effect would certainly have been strengthened when a bite from one of these creatures resulted in a rapid and painful death!

"man-eaters" such as lions, crocodiles, and sharks are regarded with awe rather than the fear and abhorrence applied to serpents.

In spite of this, snakes fascinate a great number of people. You only have to visit a public reptile collection in a zoo to observe how many visitors gawk with wonder and trepidation at the snakes through the glass of their secure enclosures. An increasing number of forward-thinking people have overcome or are overcoming their fear of snakes. There are those who like to call themselves herpetoculturists, people who study reptiles and often want to keep them as pets. I always hesitate to use the word pet when applying it to reptiles, as it implies that the animal is one that you hold in your lap while you cuddle and stroke it. Most snakes are certainly not content to be cuddled and stroked, but we will continue to use the word pet for want of a better word.

Let us take a brief look at some of the facts and characteristics of snakes in general before we go on to discuss their captive husbandry.

Photo by W. Wüster.

This coral snake, *Micrurus frontalis*, is being milked for venom that can be used to produce antivenin and other medicines.

As this photo of a Borneo Short-Tailed Python, *Python curtus breitensteini*, shows, even nonvenomous snakes can have nasty fangs.

Photo by Isabelle Francais

LIZARD OR SNAKE?

Snakes are members of the suborder Serpentes, contained in the order Squamata, which they share with another suborder Sauria, the lizards (there is another suborder Amphisbaenia, with which we are not concerned here). Thus lizards and snakes are reasonably closely related.

The differences between snakes and lizards are subtle. Probably the major difference is in the structure of the jawbones. In snakes the joints of the jaws both where they attach to the back of the skull and at the chin are held together with elastic tissue that allows an extremely large gape and gives the snake the advantage of being able to swallow prey that may sometimes be several times the diameter of its own head. This is an economical method of

Photo by David Dube.

The Ball Python, *Python regius*, probably is the most popular python. This individual demonstrates the defensive behavior of rolling up into a ball.

feeding that often provides a snake with several standard meals in one go and gives it the ability to fast for long periods between meals without losing condition.

"What about the fact that lizards have limbs, and snakes don't?," you may ask. Well, although all snakes are limbless, there are quite a few lizards that also lack external limbs and these can look just like snakes unless you examine them closely. However, many of these legless lizards have moveable eyelids and external ear openings that also are absent in snakes. In place of a moveable eyelid the snake has a hard, transparent brille or spectacle that protects the eye and gives the eye that typical, serpentine, unblinking, fierce, staring appearance.

A typical snake has a long, lithe, body and a long, tapering tail. Its numerous vertebrae have special accessory articulating facets that allow the serpent to bend its body considerably in most directions. Thus a snake can stretch itself out, coil itself up, or even wind itself into a tight ball (the Ball Python, *Python regius*, is an excellent example of this ability).

The snake's method of locomotion is one that has attracted much conjecture for generations. By just observing a snake moving it is extremely difficult to see just how it does it; it seems to simply flow across the substrate. There are in fact several methods by which snakes can move. There is the concertina movement in which the body is extended and retracted. There is the rectilinear movement in which a combination of ribs, muscles, and belly scales moves in alternating waves along the body, allowing the belly scales to drag the snake along against imperfections in the surface over which it is moving. Then there is snaking itself, in which the reptile wriggles its body and presses its flanks against objects and thus launches itself forward; this method is used in conjunction with the other types of locomotion, principally when it is in a hurry such as when it is trying to escape a predator or is chasing prey. A final interesting mode of locomotion known as sidewinding is practiced by some desert-dwelling snakes that find difficulty in moving over loose, shifting sands by the more conventional methods. Sidewinding consists of first throwing a loop of the central body forward before bringing the head and tail forward.

FEEDING WITHOUT HANDS

Various snake species have colonized suitable habitats on most of the earth's surface, with the exception of the cold polar and montane regions and some isolated islands. There are snakes that are exclusively fossorial (burrowing), some that are

Many authorities believe the monitor lizards (family Varanidae) to by the closest relatives of the snakes. This is a Gillen's Dwarf Monitor, *Varanus gilleni.*

Photo by Aaron Norman.

Despite the fact that this animal is legless, the external ear opening and the movable eyelid identify it as a lizard, not a snake. It is an Eastern Glass Lizard, *Ophisaurus ventralis*.

partially fossorial and terrestrial, and some that are quite terrestrial. There are others that are partially or wholly arboreal. Most arboreal snakes have keeled scales that help them get a better grip on bark and foliage and have prehensile tails that allow them to anchor themselves safely when feeding or resting. There are semiaquatic watersnakes and totally marine sea snakes, the latter having flattened tails that act as rudders and propellers. With a few exceptions, true sea snakes never come out on land, even giving birth to live young in the water.

All snakes are exclusively carnivorous, most of them feeding on live prey items that are subdued by various means before being swallowed. While many snakes are non-specific in their food selection, feeding on a wide variety of prey, there are others that are quite specialized in the items they eat. The fact that there are venomous snakes is a well-known fact. What is less well known is that only about ten percent of all the 3000 or so snake species are venomous, and of these only a small percentage can be considered dangerously venomous to humans. In spite of the many tall tales and exaggerations about venomous snakes that abound, the vast majority of venomous snakes are more scared of us than we are of them and would rather make themselves scarce than get into a confrontation with us. Most cases of venomous snake bites occur when the snake is deliberately or accidentally restrained.

The real purpose of a snake's venom is to subdue its prey and make it safe to swallow. As no venomous snake makes a habit of eating people (nor, of course, is any venomous snake large enough to even begin swallowing even a child), the venom would be wasted if used on us, so the snake will use its venom apparatus only as a last resort if it feels threatened. If venomous snakes use their venom to subdue their prey, what do nonvenomous species do to get the same effect?

Many snakes that feed on small, defenseless fishes, frogs, salamanders, or small lizards generally do not need to do much subduing. All they do is practice the grab and swallow method, simply grabbing the prey in the mouth and swallowing it. In most cases the act of being grabbed in the snake's sharp, recurved teeth is enough to subdue this kind of prey through shock. Nonvenomous snakes that feed on larger prey, especially mammals, have to subdue their prey by alternative means. Some mammals have very sharp teeth and strong jaws that could quickly damage a snake if the prey were not sufficiently subdued. All booids and many colubrid snakes use the system of

The Boa Constrictor, *Boa constrictor*, may be the best known constrictor; they usually make very docile pets. This one is using its cork-bark hiding place.

Photo by Isabelle Francais

Photo by Karl H. Switak

Face-to-face with an albino Burmese Python, *P. molurus bivittatus*. Notice the heat-sensitive labial pits and the opening for the tongue.

constriction to subdue the prey. This consists of grabbing the prey in the mouth and simultaneously throwing several coils of the body around it. Increasing pressure from the muscular coils will stop the prey from respiring and it soon dies from suffocation. Some kind of instinct in the snake helps it push the dangerous parts of the prey into a position where they cannot be used.

ORGANS AND SENSES

What about the snake's insides? Surprisingly to some, perhaps, snakes have much the same internal organs that we also have although, of course, they are modified to fit into an elongated cavity. Heart, liver, kidneys, and so on are all there! However, most snakes have only one large functional lung, the other being vestigial or absent.

How did snakes originate? Although they are limbless, they are classed as tetrapods (four-legged animals). This may sound bizarre, but the theory is that snakes evolved from lizard ancestors many millions of years ago. Certain lizards gradually took to a fossorial way of life, and selection for burrowing activities over countless generations resulted in the animals losing their limbs, their external ear openings, and, almost, their eyes, which became vestigial. After millions of years some of these "new" snakes began to recolonize the surface. As they had no limbs, they had to devise the typical serpentine method of moving about. The eyes redeveloped, but without moveable lids. The fact that the eye structure of snakes is quite different from that of lizards adds further weight to the theory.

One of the most amazing and fascinating aspects of the snake is its tongue, used in conjunction with the Jacobson's organ. The snake's chief sense is its sense of smell, though it smells in a different way from most other animals (many lizards also use the same method but in a less developed form). Although snakes are suspected of being able to detect scents via the nostrils, as do most other terrestrial vertebrates, they can do it even better by using the tongue and the olfactory organ situated on the palate adjacent to, but not connected with, the nasal passage. The active snake's forked tongue is continually flickering in and out through the labial notch (a little hole between the snout and the lower lip that saves the snake from opening its mouth every time it sticks its tongue out). By waving the tongue tips about in the air or over the substrate, it picks up scent particles. These are taken back into the mouth, where the tongue

The sense of smell is probably the most important sense for a snake. This King Cobra, *Ophiophagus hannah*, is "smelling" the air with its forked tongue.

Photo by Isabelle Francais.

The beautiful Rainbow Boa, *Epicrates cenchria*, like other members of its genus, has heat-sensitive pits in its labial scales.

tips are placed in the double-chambered Jacobson's organ. This extremely sensitive organ can detect minute scents and pass messages via nerves to the brain. Snakes are able to find prey, detect water, search for mates, and possibly even sense danger using this device!

A few snakes, including some of the boas and pythons and all of the pit vipers, have an even more sophisticated means of detecting warm-blooded prey. These are heat-sensitive pits lined with epithelial tissue. In the booids that have them, they lie in a row along the upper or lower labial (lip) scales either within them or between them. In the pit vipers a pit is situated between the eye and the nostril on each side of the head. These pits enable the snakes to detect and strike accurately at warm-blooded prey even in pitch darkness. Experiments have shown that the sensitive epithelial tissue in the pits is capable of detecting temperature differences of fractions of a degree of temperature!

Many breeders house their snakes in sweater boxes with ventilation holes drilled in the sides. With this type of housing, heat tape can be run across each shelf, reducing the number of separate heating units needed.

HOUSING PET SNAKES

Housing for snakes can be as simple or as elaborate as you wish. There are no hard and fast rules other than it must be escape-proof and must provide all of the appropriate environmental conditions for the species being kept.

minimum 20-gallon tank if at all possible. The tank must be fitted with a secure lid. Various types of screened lids are available on the market that can be fitted with locking devices or catches of various kinds. Make sure they are secure, as an escaped snake can

Photo by Isabelle Francais

This enclosure for a Sinaloan Milk Snake, *Lampropeltis triangulum sinaloae*, is basic, yet attractive. Water bowl, climbing branch, and hiding place are all included.

GLASS TANKS

Aquarium tanks of the type designed to keep fish are usually the first option for the beginner to snake keeping. The size of the tank will depend on the size of the snakes being kept, but a good general rule is that the length of the tank should be not less than the length of the snake. Thus a ten-gallon tank would accommodate a 24-in/60-cm snake, though it would really be better to start out with a

cause all sorts of problems with your family and even worse ones with your neighbors! If you are keeping a large snake in a large tank, you are advised to have the screening made of small gauge metal mesh. Always think about security! Snakes have an uncanny knack of getting out through holes that you would not imagine they could get through. In my early days of snake keeping I learned this lesson several times!

PLASTIC CAGES

The small plastic cages with ventilated lids that are available in pet shops have many uses. They can be used as rearing cages for baby snakes or as cages for very small species. In any case, if you intend to keep a collection of snakes it is always advisable to have a few of these tanks in various sizes for use in emergencies as isolation cages, rearing cages, etc.

WOODEN CAGES

Many snake keepers like to use special display cages made from wood and glass or plexiglass. These are especially useful when you intend to keep large pythons or boas. A glass tank of a size suitable for an adult Burmese Python, *Python molurus bivittatus*, for example, would be so heavy that you wouldn't be able to move it about! The rule for having the cage at least as long as the snake is not so important with large pythons and boas, which are very sedentary, and in any case, it would be difficult to provide 20 feet/6.15 m of cage length for a 20-foot/6.15-m snake! If you want to give these big snakes adequate space it is best to provide them with their own room rather than confine them to a cage, though of course this has its own problems.

Big snakes up to 20 feet/6.15 m will do well in a cage that is about 8 ft long by 4 ft deep by 6 ft high/2.5 by 1.25 by 1.8 m. It will probably do them good to be able to stretch themselves out completely from time to time, so an exercise period is recommended—though it must

Having a hiding place is important for a snake's psychological well-being. This albino Ruthven's Kingsnake, *Lampropeltis ruthveni*, has been given a naturalistic plastic hide-box, available at many pet stores.

Photo by Isabelle Francais

Photo by Isabelle Francais.

This rough piece of wood provides for climbing, hiding, and shedding. A "candy cane" albino Corn Snake, *Elaphe guttata*, climbs across it. However, be aware that bark provides plenty of hiding places for mites.

remembered that all snakes over about 12 feet/3 m should be considered too dangerous to handle alone. Of course, if it is impossible for you to supply such large accommodations, then stick to snake species that don't become monsters when they grow up!

Many hobbyists build their own large display cages using a variety of new and recycled materials. Other hobbyists prefer to purchase their cages or have them specially designed and built to their specifications. Unless you are handy and have quite an array of tools available, it might be best to consider a pre-made cage. Many builders advertise in the reptile magazines, and recently the pet shops have had more large cages on display, often working with local builders to provide a variety of cages and special orders.

STOCK CAGES

Stock cages are used by breeders who have to accommodate quite a lot of juvenile snakes. Most breeders opt for custom-built breeding racks made to take numbers of plastic cages and shoe boxes or sweater boxes. The shelves in the racks are designed so that the boxes just slide in between them like drawers, the upper shelf thus acting as a lid for the cage. You must ensure, of course, that the gap between the top edge of the cage and the upper shelf is almost non-existent, bearing in mind that all snakes are accomplished escape artists. You will have to drill a series of small ventilation holes in the sides of the boxes.

BEDDING

Bedding or substrate materials, call them what you will, come in many and varied forms. What you use will often have a bearing on the time or inclination you may have for frequent changing or cleaning. If time is not on your side, I would definitely recommend that you go for the simplest of bedding and furnishings in your cages! The simplest type of bedding, and indispensable for stock cages, is several layers of newspaper. This is cheap, absorbent, and easy to change each time it becomes soiled. If you don't like the look of newspaper, go for kitchen toweling, which is even better but more expensive. Paper can easily be folded to size, and two or three layers usually are adequate.

I like to use terry-cloth bath towels as floor coverings in some of my display cages. These are relatively cheap, washable, reusable, easy to fold to any size, and quite attractive to look at, especially if you go for browns or greens; if you feel inclined to go for cartoon characters or surfing designs, that is entirely up to you, but not for me!

Shingle (smooth pebble-type gravel), which is available in various grades, has long been an attractive favorite for the cage substrate. Its downside is that it has to be taken out, sterilized, and washed at frequent intervals, which is a bit labor-intensive when compared to changing newspaper. In general you can use a small grade (pea gravel) for smaller snakes and a larger grade

Aspen wood shavings make a good bedding material for many snake species like this desert-phase California Kingsnake, *Lampropeltis getula californiae*.

Photo by Isabelle Francais

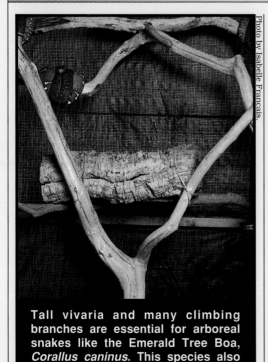

Photo by Isabelle Francais.

Tall vivaria and many climbing branches are essential for arboreal snakes like the Emerald Tree Boa, *Corallus caninus*. This species also requires high humidity.

for some of the giants.

Several types of commercial bedding are available. These range from various kinds of bark chippings through orchid compost and other specially formulated materials. These commercial products are generally safe for your snakes (but never use cedar chips of any type because of the volatile oils they emit) and are especially suitable for those species that like to partially bury themselves. Aspen bedding seems to be especially popular at the moment. If you keep desert-dwelling snakes you may opt for coarse sand as a substrate, but never use very fine sand. I have found that fine sand may cake on the skin of some snakes after they have crawled through the water bath, resulting in shedding problems.

ROCKS AND BRANCHES

These add to the esthetics of the cage interior, provide starting points for snakes to shed, and give them exercise by providing added dimensions for them to climb on, over, or under. Don't clutter the cage with too many rocks and branches, however; this only makes more cleaning work. A good solid rock and a branch of reasonable size should be adequate. Rocks and branches can be obtained in some pet stores. You can even get artificial rocks and branches with premade hollows for your snakes to hide in. However, my personal preference is for natural rocks and logs that I have collected myself. A good place to look is along river banks, where you are likely to find rocks and branches that have been nicely weathered. Wherever you get the items you use, you should wash and scrub them thoroughly and dry them out before use. For arboreal snakes you should use taller branches that can be fastened to the top of the cage and allow adequate climbing room. All rocks and logs should be placed in a secure position in the cage or fastened so that the danger of them falling and injuring the snakes is reduced.

PLANTS

A naturalistic snake terrarium with living plants is a challenge. Plants often are more difficult to keep healthy in a cage than the snakes themselves. It is advisable to use living plants only in cages with small, light-weight snakes. Heavy snakes soon crush plants, causing them damage from which they will take a long time to recover. Of course you could always use a tough plastic plant or two!

If you want a snake display with living plants, use plant species that are classed as tough house plants. Remember that the plants will need good quality light if they are to survive. Plants are best left in their pots, which can be disguised behind logs, rocks, or cork bark. Keep a couple of spare sets of plants so that you can change them around at intervals. This will allow plants from the terrarium to spend a period of "recovery" in the windowsill or in the greenhouse.

HIDE BOXES

Most snake species will be less likely to be stressed, especially in their early stages of captivity, if they are given some kind of a hide box. This can range from a simple cardboard food carton (which can be discarded and replaced when necessary) through various kinds of plastic containers with holes cut in the sides, if you plan on recycling materials to your cage. Very attractive wooden hide boxes and hollowed out logs, as well as ceramic hide boxes in a variety of shapes, sizes, and colors, are available from your pet shop.

WATER BATHS

All snake species should have

This young female Jungle Carpet Python, *Python spilota cheynei*, has a nicely furnished cage, complete with water bowl, hiding place, and aspen bedding.

Photo by Isabelle Francais.

Photo by Isabelle Francais.

The Kenyan Sand Boa, *Eryx colubrinus loveridgei*, does quite well when housed on sand. Make sure you use a sand that is safe for reptiles. Ask pet store personnel for a recommendation.

access to a permanent supply of fresh drinking water. Some species like to bathe at regular intervals. Use heavy containers if possible (stoneware dog dishes are excellent and come in various sizes) so that the snakes cannot tip them over. For larger snakes you may have to use something like a plastic dish tub or a baby bath weighted down by placing a clean brick or rock in the base. Water must be changed frequently as it becomes soiled. If you don't change it, not only will it smell horribly, it could become a source of disease! Always make sure the replacement water has had the chill taken out of it.

TEMPERATURE

Most snakes will require some form of supplementary heating in the confines of the terrarium.

Because snakes are cold-blooded, or ectothermic, they are very sensitive to temperature changes. They all have a preferred range of body temperatures that they maintain by moving in or out of warmed areas if given the chance. It thus is important to provide your snakes with a temperature gradient in the cage so that they can warm or cool themselves as they require. This is achieved by placing the heater at one end of the cage. It is, of course, preferable to provide your snakes with the ranges of temperatures that they would enjoy in their natural habitats. If you know where your snake species originates, then you can look at a good quality world atlas and find out about the climate to which it is accustomed.

In most parts of the world a

temperature reduction at night is natural. This can be achieved in the terrarium simply by switching off the heaters in the evening and turning them on again in the morning. In most homes the normal night temperature is quite sufficient, but if you keep your snakes in a cold shed or garage, you may have to supply them with some form of weak heating at night to keep out the chill.

Seasonal temperature fluctuations also are considered to be important. In general, tropical areas are fairly temperature constant throughout the year, but in the subtropical and temperate regions temperature reductions at night and from season to season can be quite dramatic. Seasonal fluctuations in temperature play an important part in the breeding cycles of many species, especially those that hibernate during the colder winter months. In captivity it generally is not necessary to provide complete hibernation conditions; a couple of months at reduced temperature is all that is usually required to attain satisfactory breeding results.

Various types of heating apparatus are available, all of which have their uses. Simple incandescent light bulbs can be used for small to medium sized cages. They come in various wattages and they give off a fair amount of heat as well as some supplementary light. Experiment with a thermometer and various bulb wattages until you come up with the right temperature range. By using a reflector, you can direct the heat downward onto a

particular basking spot in the cage. Spot lamps with built-in reflectors come in various sizes and can be used in a similar manner. Some of these are ceramic coated and emit heat only, without light. When using bulbs, lamps, or other radiant heat emitters, be sure that the snakes cannot get into direct contact with them or even too close to them. Snakes can be severely burned by lying next to heat sources! Lamps used to warm basking sites preferably should be located above the cage, with the beam directed through the screening. For reasons of safety, ensure that the surface of a basking spot never exceeds 100°F/38°C. You can do this by using a thermometer in the basking spot and by raising or lowering the heat source until the desired temperature is reached.

Other heating devices include heating cables that can be placed in some types of substrate, heating pads or boards that can be placed beneath terraria, and heating tapes that can be used almost anywhere. Always remember to leave an unheated spot in the terrarium to allow snakes to cool down should they feel too warm. Heated rocks generally are not suitable for use in snake cages. They usually are not large enough to warm up the whole snake at once, and there have been reports of them causing burns.

PHOTOPERIOD AND LIGHTING

Under natural conditions the sun is the primary source of light as well as heat, and these two factors should go hand in hand in the terrarium. A natural photoperiod is the amount of time each day in which the sun provides light. During the winter in certain parts of the temperate regions, for example, the sun may be up for only eight hours during each 24-hour period. The photoperiod in the subtropics, depending on the latitude, may be ten hours, while in equatorial regions photoperiod is more or less a constant 12 hours throughout the year. When providing our captive snakes with seasonal temperature variations it is important to vary the photoperiod as well.

These variations generally do not have to be precisely the same as those of the native habitat, and compromises can be made. Tropical species can be kept with a 12-hour photoperiod throughout the year. For subtropical to southern temperate species the photoperiod can be 13 hours in summer and 11 hours in winter, while for northern temperate species this can be 15 hours in summer and nine hours in winter. Changing from summer to winter photoperiod (and temperature), or vice versa, should be done gradually over a

couple of weeks, not suddenly. A winter regime also will include a reduction in feeding.

Unlike many diurnal basking lizards, it seems that most snakes are less dependent on broad-spectrum lighting (as in natural daylight), but many herpetoculturists feel that their snakes also should be given the benefits of this commodity. Broad-spectrum artificial lighting is becoming ever-more sophisticated, and there are brands of lamps available that are specially manufactured for terraria. It will be worth shopping around in your local pet shops or looking in herp magazines to see what is on the market. Read the manufacturer's specifications before making your decision on what to use.

Photo by Isabelle Francais.

Record-keeping is important, especially if you plan to breed your animals. Eating, shedding, and mating, as well as disease and odd behavior, should be kept track of.

AUTOMATIC CONTROLS

It would be very convenient if you could work your heating and lighting controls automatically. A system of timers, dimmers, thermostats, rheostats, and so on will save you a lot of time. If you are not electrically or electronically minded, get someone to help you who is. Always use good quality equipment and don't mess around with wiring unless you really know what you're doing!

The gorgeous Mexican Kingsnake, *Lampropeltis mexicana mexicana*, will thrive if housed in a warm and dry terrarium.
Photo by Isabelle Francais

WHAT TO FEED SNAKES

Before actually discussing individual food items, let us first examine the mechanisms by which snakes find their prey. All snakes are carnivorous, which means that they eat animal as opposed to vegetable food. The only vegetable food a snake may consume is what may accidentally be picked up during the swallowing of the prey or may be contained, undigested, in the gut of a herbivorous prey animal.

Snakes are famous for the fact that they generally feed on whole prey animals and that they are capable of swallowing prey several times larger than their own heads. Snakes are indeed unable to tear or chew their prey, so they must swallow it whole. One big advantage of being able to capture, overpower, and swallow whole prey is that the snake gets a complete balanced meal in a single package that often is large enough to provide it with nutrition for several days or even weeks.

Photo by Paul Freed.

Beware! Many snakes will eat other snakes. This Texas Coral Snake, *Micrurus fulvius tener*, dines on a Rough Earth Snake, *Virginia striatula*.

However, in spite of the fact that snakes do swallow what to us are amazingly large items, there are many exaggerated stories in circulation. Tales about anacondas or large pythons overpowering and swallowing animals as large as cows can be taken with a pinch of salt!

While most snakes are more or less generalized feeders taking a variety of prey, there are some that specialize in certain food items. Some normally will eat only frogs, others favor lizards in their diets. A few snakes, such as the King Cobra, *Ophiophagus hannah*, feed almost exclusively on other snakes. There are other snakes that specialize in eating eggs, and yet others that eat only snails or centipedes, just to give a few examples.

Some of the more specialized feeders are not popular captives due to the problems in feeding them, though some can eventually be persuaded to change their diet. A salamander-eater, for example,

Many snakes include frogs and toads in their natural diet, and some even eat nothing else. This Toad Adder, *Causus rhombeatus*, demonstrates how it got its name.

often can be converted to a mouse- eater by giving it salamander- flavored mice! Unfortunately, you will need a few salamanders to start off with. These are killed and pureed, and the mice then are dipped in the salamander essence before being fed to the snakes. The amount of essence is reduced over a period of a few weeks until the snake accepts just the mice.

RATS, MICE, AND CHICKS

By far the majority of snakes kept by hobbyists are mouse- or rat-eaters, or at least they will readily accept these as food items. Boas and pythons, ratsnakes, kingsnakes, and other popular types are good examples. This is very convenient, as mice and rats are about the easiest snake food items to obtain and usually are in fairly continuous supply. Many companies supply mice or rats, dead or alive and in various sizes from pinkies to adults, to suit various sized snakes. Dead ones can be bought frozen so they can be kept in the freezer and thawed out to room temperature as necessary. It is most convenient to get your snakes to eat dead prey if at all possible. As most snakes kill live prey in the wild, it may take a while to persuade some of them to eat dead prey. This usually can be done by placing a dead mouse or rat in front of the snake's mouth and jiggling it about. Use a thin stick

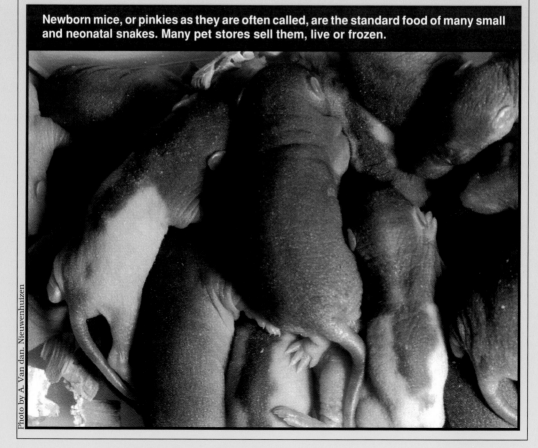

Newborn mice, or pinkies as they are often called, are the standard food of many small and neonatal snakes. Many pet stores sell them, live or frozen.

Photo by Isabelle Francais.

Caught in the act! This Corn Snake, *E. guttata*, strikes a mouse. Notice that the snake bites the head of the mouse. This behavior keeps the mouse from biting the snake during constriction.

to do this (a bamboo kebab skewer is ideal) so in case the snake misses the prey it will not get your hand by mistake! Initially the snake may be irritated by your attempts to get it to feed, but once it gets a taste of the offering it usually will continue to swallow it.

Some hobbyists elect to keep their own breeding colonies of mice or rats, but this can be very time-consuming. If you do want to do this, remember to treat the animals kindly and humanely and don't neglect them just because they are snake food!

Another food that is widely used for snakes is chickens. Day-old chicks may be available in frozen batches. For large snakes, chickens in various sizes of growth can be used. For large Burmese and Reticulated Pythons, Anacondas, and Boa Constrictors, adult chickens are about the most convenient food. Of course, the chickens must be whole and fully feathered; don't try to use frozen roasters from the supermarket!

FISHES AND OTHERS

For many small snakes, especially water snakes, garter snakes, etc., fishes are a preferred item. Goldfish, guppies, killifishes, and other cheap and easy to breed varieties usually are available. Fishes are mostly fed alive, but some snakes will take them dead. To ensure an adequate diet, give only whole

Photo by W. P. Mara.

If feeding your snake large amounts of fish, use a vitamin supplement regularly, because fish are often low in B vitamins. This is the Mangrove Salt Marsh Snake, *Nerodia clarki compressicauda*

fishes and use only freshwater fishes.

Small insect- eating snakes, such greensnakes, can be fed on a variety of collected or cultured live invertebrate foods. Crickets are very convenient, as are the larvae of the wax moth. Both of these are available commercially and also are quite easy to breed if you feel so inclined. Earthworms are another prey item often used to feed such species as garter snakes.

SUPPLEMENTS

As most snakes take whole prey animals, vitamin/mineral supplements are not normally necessary. Occasionally a veterinarian will recommend a course of supplements for a snake that is in poor condition for one reason or another. If the snake is feeding it is quite easy to inject a suitable dose of a liquid vitamin/ mineral supplement into the dead prey animal before it is fed to the snake.

AMOUNT TO FEED

Use common sense when feeding snakes. Some individuals are literally eating machines and will consume almost anything you care to put in front of them. An obese snake is an unhealthy one. It will build up excessive amounts of fat around the internal organs and these will then be unable to function properly. Obese snakes will die young and will be next to

This Ball Python, *P. regius*, is being offered a pinky. The use of forceps or tongs prevents being bitten.
Photo by Isabelle Francais.

useless for breeding purposes. Ensure your snakes remain lithe and fit, and should any signs of overweight become evident, cut back on the meals. As a general guide, a mouse-eating snake should be given no more than two mice per week. Subtropical and temperate species should have a winter "rest period" at reduced temperature and photoperiod for a couple of months. During this time feeding is stopped and restarted only when the rest period is over. It will do no harm to any well-fed snake if it is given an occasional week without food. A good regimen is to feed them weekly for four weeks, then to miss a week.

FORCE FEEDING

Occasionally you may come across a snake that will inexplicably refuse to eat anything you have to offer it. There are some notoriously difficult feeders. In this connection Ball Pythons, *Python regius*, come to mind, especially wild-caught specimens. I have found that putting the snake in a dark bag along with a dead mouse overnight often will result in the snake eating it. In any case, always provide your snake with a hide box—the security of having a safe haven from which to launch an attack seems to be a good starting point for difficult feeders.

Force feeding should be carried out as a last resort when all else fails. Try to ascertain why the snake isn't feeding. Are you giving it the right prey? Is it sick? It won't harm to have it examined by a good reptile veterinarian who may be able to diagnose and treat the sickness. The treatment may include a course of force feeding. There are a couple of ways you can force feed a snake.

To force feed a whole dead mouse to a snake, open the snake's mouth by gently but firmly pulling down on the loose skin below the jaw. Push the mouse's head into the snake's mouth and work it in as far as you can. Often the snake will bite into the mouse immediately and will continue to swallow it once you release it. In some cases you will have to work the mouse right down into the gullet. Once the mouse's body is engulfed, you can push it down into the snake's gullet using a smooth rod (the handle of a wooden spoon lubricated with a little cooking oil is ideal). Once the mouse is past the snake's neck, you can gently massage it down into the stomach.

Another method of force feeding is to administer liquid food via a syringe and a smooth-ended stomach tube. The dead food item is first liquefied in a blender and then put in the syringe; you may need to add some water to make the liquid free-running. Take the snake in one hand and push the end of the tube into the snake's labial notch. The tube should pass about one-third of the way down the snake's body before you slowly squeeze out the contents of the syringe. So that all of the food is pushed out of the pipe, you can put some water in the syringe above the food.

Hatchling Gray-banded Kingsnakes, *Lampropeltis mexicana alterna*, are sometimes difficult to feed. Try offering lizards and lizard-scented pinkies.

Photo by Isabelle Francais.

ASPECTS OF SNAKE BREEDING

The prospects of breeding snakes in captivity no longer hold the mystique that they held in the past. At one time breeding was the exception more than the rule, and captive births, more often than not, arose only from wild females that were gravid at capture.

Today, with our increased knowledge of the conditions required to bring snakes into breeding condition, most species can be encouraged to reproduce successfully, though there are some species that remain "difficult."

IDENTIFICATION OF THE SEXES

It is not generally easy to identify the sexes of most snake species just by looking at them, and there are no hard and fast rules for all snake species. The following list of points shows some of the sexual differences that may occur in many species, but these, of course, will only be useful if you have enough comparative material.

1. Adult female snakes usually are somewhat larger and more robust than their corresponding males (but there are a few exceptions).

2. Female snakes often have a shorter tail than their male counterparts. Subcaudal scale counts are thus often greater in males than in females (again, there may be some exceptions).

3. Male snakes often show a thickening of the tail base. This indicates the presence of the inverted hemipenes, the male sex organs.

4. In some booid species the anal "claws" or "spurs" often are larger and/or longer in males than in females.

A fairly modern and successful technique for sexing snakes is known as genital probing. This involves using a "sexing probe" of appropriate size. Sexing probes are ball-tipped rods that may be obtained in sets containing various sizes from herpetological suppliers. To sex a snake, the smooth ball tip of the probe is first sterilized in boiling water and cooled, then lubricated with a little mineral oil. It is inserted into the cloaca at either side and pushed very gently in the direction of the tail. If the snake is a male, the probe should enter the withdrawn hemipenis and pass unhindered to a distance the equivalent of 7-10 (and often many more) subcaudal scales. In a female it cannot be pushed more than a distance of 1-3 subcaudals. Probing should be carried out with the utmost caution; never try and force it as you are likely to injure the snake. It may require some practice before you are proficient. If at all possible, get an experienced "prober" to show you how to do it.

Photo by Isabelle Francais.

The hemipenes of a male Borneo Short-tailed Python, *P. c. breitensteini*, are fully extended and visible on this specimen.

BREEDING CYCLES

Most snakes breed once, sometimes twice per annum. Their breeding cycles are influenced by climatic conditions. Temperature, photoperiod, and humidity all may play an important part in bringing snakes into breeding condition. These seasonal influences help snakes to produce sex hormones that excite them into sexual activity.

In temperate and subtropical climates most snakes spend all or part of the winter in hibernation, the length of time depending on how long and cold the winter is at their particular location. There is evidence to suggest that this period of cooling also plays a part in the breeding cycles of many species. Some temperate species kept constantly warm throughout the year will not attempt to breed.

Most snakes that live in tropical climates seem to mate during the dry season. This is important for oviparous species, as the eggs can then be laid when the wet season starts so that they have adequate moisture to develop. The eggs hatch in the wet season when there is an abundance of prey for the hatchlings, giving them a good start in life. Even most viviparous species seem to "time" the birth of their young in the wet season for similar reasons.

MATING BEHAVIOR

Having come into breeding condition under the influence of climatic conditions, male snakes will actively seek out females. It is at this time that many normally secretive snakes are most obvious to human observers, giving rise to such reports as "snake plagues" or the "snake season is upon us." Sexually receptive females release

Probing is the most reliable way of sexing a snake. Most snakes, like this Ball Python, *P. regius*, require two people to probe.

Photo by Isabelle Francais

pheromones from tiny glands in the skin between the scales. These pheromones are highly attractive to male snakes, which are able to pick up the scent from some distance away and to "home in" on it by the use of their olfactory senses (forked tongue and Jacobson's organ).

Sometimes two or more males arrive on the scene at the same time. In some cases this gives rise to male combat, which varies from species to species. It may consist of a sort of minor wrestling match in which the rival males twist their bodies together; eventually the less powerful adversaries will give up and try their luck elsewhere. Other forms of combat include a type of serpentine arm wrestling; the two opponents rear up against each other and each endeavors to push the other's head to the ground. In nature

Photo by Isabelle Francais.

To prevent the transmission of disease, always wipe probes with alcohol before and after each use. Also, lubricate the probe before insertion.

This Burmese Python, *P. molurus bivittatus*, probably is a male, given the distance the probe has entered the cloaca.

Photo by Isabelle Francais.

serious injuries are rare, but in captivity males, especially booids, sometimes may injure each other seriously with their teeth (deep flesh lacerations). This is mostly due to the fact that the vanquished snake has no means of making itself scarce in the confines of a cage.

Male to female snake courtship is fairly consistent from one species to the next. In a typical case, once a male finds himself in close proximity to a sexually attractive female he will become increasingly excited, showing jerky body movements and vigorous tongue flicking. He approaches the female and moves alongside her body, "tasting" her pheromones with his tongue, often paying particular attention to her cloacal region. A non-receptive female may take exception to his advances and try to escape his attentions, but if the female is receptive she will lie passively while he crawls along her body. Eventually he will get into a position where his cloacal area is adjacent to hers and will push his tail beneath hers (sometimes the female will oblige by lifting her tail) so that he can insert one of his engorged hemipenes into her cloaca.

Copulation may last for a few minutes to several hours depending in the species and the conditions. Sperm are passed along a groove in the hemipenis and deposited in the female's cloaca, from whence they make their way along the oviducts to fertilize her eggs before the tough outer shell is formed. Some female snakes can retain viable sperm in their bodies for quite long periods, in some cases up to seven years. This explains why occasional

This Speckled Kingsnake, *Lampropeltis getula holbrooki*, has laid her eggs in damp sphagnum moss. Having a nesting box half-full of sphagnum moss will help prevent both egg-binding and scattering of the eggs.

Photo by Isabelle Francais

These healthy eggs from a Speckled Kingsnake are incubating on a vermiculite substrate, which is available at most gardening stores.

isolated captive females lay fertile eggs or give birth months or even years after capture.

GETTING A BREEDING RESPONSE

Herpetoculturists use various methods to bring their captive snakes into breeding condition. There are no hard and fast rules, and some keepers will swear by one method, while others may discount the same one. There seems little doubt that temperate region snakes will benefit from a short period of winter hibernation at a cooler temperature, coupled with a reduction of photoperiod. Feeding should be stopped in late fall and the temperature gradually reduced by a couple of degrees each day over a period of about

two weeks. At the same time the daily photoperiod should be reduced by about 15 minutes each day. Once the temperature and photoperiod have been reduced to the required level, the cages should be left in an unheated room (but the ambient temperature should not be allowed to fall below 50°F/10°C) for a couple of months. At the end of this period the temperature and photoperiod can be brought back to summer levels using the reverse procedure.

Subtropical and tropical species also seem to benefit from a reduction in temperature, photoperiod, and feeding for a short period in the winter, but complete hibernation is not necessary. Winter rest period temperatures for subtropical species should not be reduced below 59°F/15°C for a period of about six weeks; tropical species should not go below 68°F/20°C for a period of about four weeks.

Sexes are best kept separately outside the breeding season. Males can be introduced to females once both sexes are again feeding after the winter rest period. In most cases courtship and copulation will occur soon after introduction. In some species two males are introduced to a single female and the masculine competition often enhances the chance of a successful mating. Keep a close eye on rival males at this time, and if things start to get too hot between them it will be best to remove one of them before any serious injury occurs. Also, as soon as one male seems to be making good progress in his courtship with the female, the other should be removed.

Leave the male and female together for a few days to allow for any subsequent matings that will improve the possibilities of a fertile clutch. Once you think the female is successfully impregnated, the male can be moved back to his permanent quarters.

THE GRAVID FEMALE

A female snake with fertile eggs is said to be gravid, rather than pregnant. All snakes develop inside eggs within the female's body. Some species lay eggs with only partially developed embryos and the eggs then have to spend a period of incubation outside the maternal body before they hatch; these species are said to be oviparous (egg-layers). In other species the embryos develop to full term in the eggs within the female's body and hatch during or shortly after deposition; these are known as ovoviviparous (livebearing) species. The eggs of oviparous species are covered with a tough, white, porous, leathery shell that protects the contents from the elements during incubation but, at the same time, also allows for gas and moisture exchange. The eggs of ovoviviparous species, however, are relatively soft, transparent, and membranous.

The period of gravidity varies from species to species and to some extent on the prevailing climatic conditions. Warmer conditions, for example, will speed the process, while cooler conditions will slow it down. The period of gravidity in oviparous species commonly is relatively shorter than that of ovoviviparous species.

Two or three weeks after a fertile mating, the gravid female will begin to show outward signs of her condition. She will begin to visibly gain weight in the posterior part of her abdomen, and after a week or two more, you may able to see and feel the bulges in her skin caused by the developing eggs. Toward the latter half of her gravid period the female usually will stop feeding. This is a natural phenomenon and there is no need to worry; she will feed again after laying her eggs. However, she may drink increasing amounts of water at this time, so ensure that fresh drinking water is always available.

OVIPOSITION

In the wild, oviparous snakes usually lay their eggs in some kind of concealed cavity. This may be under a log or rock or among loose soil, ground litter, or decaying vegetation. Most species show no further concern for their

Calloselasma rhodostoma, coils around its eggs in a scrape on the forest floor. Ovoviviparous species seem to be even less concerned about where they deposit their young, but usually they do so in a sheltered spot.

Snakes in captivity often lay their eggs haphazardly on the floor of the cage; sometimes they may even end up in the water bath. This usually is because they either have not been given any

Photo by Isabelle Francais

A simple incubator setup for incubating python eggs. These are relatively easy to make, or one could be purchased.

eggs after they have been laid. Notable exceptions include most pythons, which coil around their eggs to protect and "incubate" them. The King Cobra, *Ophiophagus hannah*, scrapes together a nest of dry, fallen leaves and other vegetation and stays close to the eggs until they hatch. The Malayan Pit Viper,

laying facilities or are not happy with the facilities you may have offered. You should keep a close watch on your snakes at this time so that eggs can be quickly collected for incubation before they spoil. As egg-laying time approaches, the female snake will become visibly restless, crawling around the cage and testing every corner with her tongue. It is advisable to provide oviparous snakes with one or two egg-laying boxes. While these may not always be used, it is safer to provide them. A good egg-laying box can be made with a plastic container (food storage box, ice cream tub, margarine tub, etc., depending upon the size of the snake). A snake-sized hole is cut in the side of the container and it is lightly stuffed with barely moist sphagnum moss. Wherever your snakes lay their eggs, they must be collected and incubated artificially. The eggs will rarely, if ever, hatch if left in the cage (an exception is the eggs of those pythons that incubate their own eggs).

It is quite simple to make an incubator for snake eggs. You can use a fish tank, plastic-foam box, or a specially made wooden box. For heating you can use heat pads or tapes, a lamp, an aquarium heater or something similar. The heat source must be thermostatically controlled so that the temperature around the eggs, for most species, is maintained at 79-86°F/26-30°C. If you use an aquarium heater in a jar of water it will help keep the humidity inside the incubator high, but you must ensure that you top up the water as necessary. It is best to use a thermistor type heat measuring device in which a temperature probe is placed near the eggs. This is connected with a wire to a temperature gauge outside the incubator, allowing you to monitor the temperature easily.

Incubating eggs of all species require adequate moisture and oxygen. Most breeders incubate snake eggs in a moisture-retaining medium, of which granular vermiculite seems to be the most widely used. This inert insulating material is highly absorbent. Initially it is mixed with an equal amount of water by volume, then any excessive water is squeezed out. Place a layer of the moist vermiculite in a plastic container with a ventilated lid, making sure that there is adequate space between the top of the medium and the lid (this is so that hatchling snakes have somewhere to go when they hatch!). The eggs should be buried to about three-quarters their depth in the medium, thus leaving about one-quarter visible. Once placed in position, it is advisable to leave them in that position throughout the period of incubation; you can mark a dot on the "top" surface of the eggs so that you know how to keep them the right way up. The lid of the incubator should be opened completely every day for just a few minutes to allow a complete air change.

Check the eggs regularly during incubation, but lift them out as little as possible; it is best to let nature take its own course. You must also monitor the temperature regularly. A slight deviation within the range suggested above will do no harm, but if you let the temperature get too low or too high there is a danger that the developing embryos will die or hatch with deformities. If you think the surface of the medium is getting too dry, you should mist the surface *very lightly* with lukewarm water.

The time it takes for the eggs to hatch will depend on the species and the temperature, but most eggs will hatch in the range of 60-100 days. If you inspect the eggs after a couple of weeks you will be able to see the blood vessels forming just below the surface of

dies in the shell. These eggs gradually discolor and spoil. Do not be in too much of a hurry to discard such eggs, as sometimes even healthy eggs can assume some alarming and unhealthy looking colors. If you are sure an egg is infertile or the embryo is dead, then you can discard it.

As hatching time approaches inspect the eggs more often. The hatchling snakes slit open the shell with their egg tooth (this is

Photo by Paul Freed.

After slitting a hole in the shell, snakes often will sit in their eggs for quite some time before fully emerging. This McGregor's Viper, *Trimeresurus mcgregori*, seems content to wait.

the shell and may be able to perceive the shadow of the developing embryo if the eggs are fertile. Healthy eggs actually absorb moisture and increase in weight during incubation, and the shell will become quite taut and springy to the touch (but don't squeeze them too hard!). In most clutches there will be one or two eggs that are either infertile or, for one reason or another, the young

situated in the snout and is cast off soon after hatching) before sticking out their heads. The actual work required for the little hatchling to open the egg is quite exhausting, and the hatchlings will often rest for several hours, breathing the atmospheric air and exercising their lungs before emerging completely. Don't try and hurry them; let them be, and they'll come out eventually.

REARING THE YOUNG

Once the neonates are completely out of the eggshell and moving about over the surface of the incubation medium, you can remove them and place them in a nursery cage. In the case of ovoviviparous species they should be taken away from the mother snake as soon as they are actively crawling about. You should keep the nursery cages simply furnished but provide the little snakes with all the necessary requirements recommended for adults. Most youngsters will not feed for the first few days, but don't worry, they still are absorbing nutrients from the yolk sac attached to the mid abdomen. As the yolk sac is absorbed, it will leave a little scar, the equivalent of the human "belly button." This will soon heal up of its own accord, and there is no need to be concerned about it.

Most youngsters do not feed until after the first skin shedding, which usually takes place in two to ten days after hatching (or live birth). Young snakes must have correspondingly small food. The young of many of the more popular colubrid species will start off on pinkie mice, while many young boids can, almost from birth, overpower and eat larger mice.

Care must be taken to provide hatchling snakes with properly sized food. It is plain to see that food for this baby *Sibynomorphus turgidus* must be tiny.

HEALTH AND SICKNESS

Until relatively recently, reptilian diseases had been studied only sparsely by the scientific community. The current growing interest in reptiles as pets, however, has led to an increasing number of veterinarians with a specialized knowledge of reptilian disorders. This means that anyone with a sick snake now stands at least half a chance of getting it professionally treated, while in the not too distant past this often was an impossibility.

PREVENTIVE HEALTH CARE

The most important aspect of keeping captive snakes healthy is to provide them with optimum, stress-free conditions and to give them an adequate diet. In the past, authors describing the difficulty of maintaining certain species put it down to "unable to adapt to captive life," but with the increased technology available and a more detailed knowledge of a species's environmental requirements there is no reason

why any species should not be able to live a healthy, long, and productive life. Even some of the more "nervous" snake species such as racers are being kept increasingly successfully.

To provide optimum captive conditions we must first have some idea of the natural habitat of the species in question, in particular with regard to the climatic and seasonal conditions. Once these conditions are reproduced in the terrarium, we have surmounted the first problem. An animal kept in suboptimum conditions will suffer stress, its metabolism will suffer, and its immune system will fail, allowing the invasion of disease organisms and the subsequent outbreak of disease.

Next to providing optimum conditions, we must consider hygiene. Hygiene is the science of disease prevention and control. Some aspects of hygiene can be quite complicated, but as far as the captive care of snakes goes it

Photo by Isabelle Francais.

It is obvious that this Sinaloan Milk Snake, *L. t. sinaloae*, has been kept in the proper environment. It seems to have adequate weight, good muscle tone, and healthy color.

is mostly common sense. Cages must be kept clean. Fecal matter should be removed as soon as possible after it appears. Water vessels should be emptied, cleaned, and replenished daily. Cages should be stripped down at least once per week and thoroughly cleaned. Substrates are either discarded or washed and replaced, depending on what they are. The cage should be cleaned both inside and out, and all furnishings should be scrubbed and disinfected. Dilute household bleach makes a good disinfectant as long as it is throughly rinsed off with clean water afterward. Never use phenol or coal-tar based disinfectants as these could be harmful to your snakes.

Put your snakes in a clean, secure container while you are cleaning out their cage. Never mix snakes from different cages, and it is advisable to wash out your spare container each time you put a new snake in it. I like to use a plastic trash can as a holding container, because it is easy to rinse out. Sanitize all cleaning equipment you use and even your hands—always wash equipment and hands thoroughly after dealing with one cage and proceeding to the next. If you have a number of cages in a snake room it is advisable to wear an

As a veterinarian familiar with reptiles can be hard to find, locate one before there is an emergency. This Ball Python, *P. regius*, is receiving antibiotics.

Photo by Isabelle Francais

Photo by Isabelle Francais.

A Corn Snake, *E. guttata*, is put in a clean garbage pail during cage cleaning. Disinfect temporary housing after each use.

apron or coveralls during servicing operations. Keep them in the snake room and take them off when you leave. Needless to say, aprons and coveralls should be laundered at frequent intervals.

Salmonellosis, a usually minor intestinal bacterial infection, recently has been in the news. This disease is carried by snakes, though it does not appear to be a major problem at the moment. Because salmonellosis is readily transferred from snake fecal matter to humans, caution is advised during any cleaning of the snake cage or any other contact with a reptile, for that matter, especially if young children, pregnant women, the elderly, or immune-compromised persons are present in the household. Wear disposable latex gloves when cleaning tanks, especially when changing water or picking up feces, and try not to ever put anything having to do with your snake anywhere near food preparation areas such as kitchen sinks. You have a much greater chance of getting salmonellosis from the supermarket chicken roaster than from your snake, but it doesn't hurt to not take chances.

QUARANTINE AND ISOLATION

These are both more or less the same thing. Any snake that becomes sick must be isolated from any other apparently healthy snakes before it infects all of them and while it is getting treatment. With regard to quarantine, this is a period of isolation that you give any new snakes you may acquire

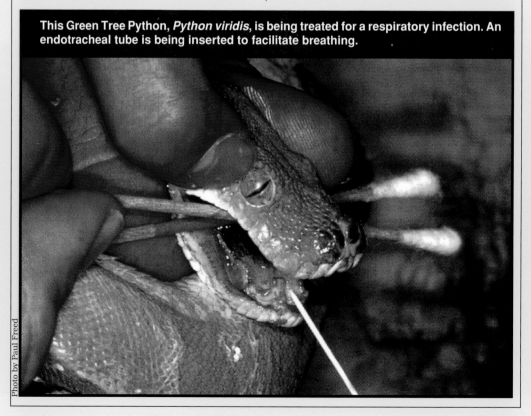

This Green Tree Python, *Python viridis*, is being treated for a respiratory infection. An endotracheal tube is being inserted to facilitate breathing.

Photo by Paul Freed

Photo by Isabelle Francais

Misting cages with lukewarm water will help maintain proper humidity. If kept too dry, these Green Tree Python hatchlings could develop respiratory and skin problems.

crop up occasionally. The following is a brief summary of the more commonly encountered ailments of captive snakes and what to do if they occur.

Mouthrot

More correctly called necrotic stomatitis, this is one of the common and debilitating problems in pet snakes, especially recently captured specimens. The problem often arises as a result of the nervous snake striking at the cage glass or continually rubbing its snout into corners in attempts to escape. This may break the skin around the snout and lips, and in some cases even the teeth and jawbones may be injured. The wounds are then invaded by pathogenic bacteria, causing

before introducing them to any of your existing stock. I would suggest a period of quarantine of about four weeks, during which you can keep an eye on the new snake and make sure it's not coming down with something nasty that it could pass on. A simply furnished quarantine cage should be kept, preferably in a separate room from your main stock. If your new snake is still healthy after four weeks, you can move it to its permanent quarters, but if it should become sick during this time you must have it treated and keep it isolated until it has been given a clean bill of health.

DISEASES AND TREATMENTS

However careful you have been in the care of your snakes, a disease of some kind or other may

Rinsing snakes with lukewarm water can facilitate molting. Be very careful not to lose hold of the snake or it could end up down the drain. This is a baby Corn Snake, *E. guttata*.

Photo by Isabelle Francais

Photo by Paul Freed

The cloudy blue eyes of this Speckled Rattlesnake, *Crotalus mitchelli mitchelli*, indicate that it is close to shedding its skin. The cloudiness is caused by fluid trapped between the old and new brilles.

inflammation, debility, loss of appetite, and eventual death unless successfully treated. Symptoms include an inability of the snake to close its mouth properly due to the swollen mucous membranes and a gray, pasty, exudate on the areas around the teeth. The problem can be largely avoided if the snake is acclimated properly, given a suitable hide box, and not disturbed too much.

Initial treatment includes the irrigation of the mouth (being sure

Ticks only rarely cause serious problems, but they are a parasite and must be disposed of. The ticks that infect snakes are not known to transmit diseases to humans.

Photo by Paul Freed

the entire insides are reached) with a mild antiseptic such as hydrogen peroxide or povidone iodine. In severe cases it is best to refer the case to a veterinarian, who may surgically remove infected tissue under general anesthetic. Treatment normally is accompanied by a course of antibiotics. It may be necessary to force feed the snake while it is undergoing treatment.

Bacterial and Protozoan Infections

A number of bacterial diseases occur in snakes. The most

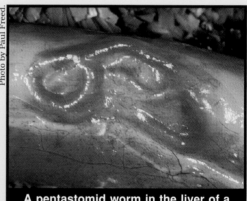

Photo by Paul Freed

A pentastomid worm in the liver of a Wagler's or Temple Viper, *Trimeresurus wagleri*. Buying captive-bred animals usually ensures that your purchase has no internal parasites.

prominent and common probably is salmonellosis. Some strains of the bacteria *Salmonella* and *Arizona*, the major causes of the disease, are infective to humans, a major reason why personal hygiene is a priority when handling reptiles. While some strains of the bacteria do not adversely affect the snake, others may result in enteric problems, manifesting themselves in severe, foul smelling diarrhea. Your veterinarian will probably advise antibiotics. The most common protozoan infection is *Entamoeba invadens*, which causes a form of dysentery. Again, veterinary treatment often is successful if the disease is caught in time.

Dysecdysis

This is as an inability to shed properly. Healthy snakes cast off their old, worn skins at irregular intervals, but usually about three to eight times a year depending on such factors as species, age, climate, and so on. The skin of a healthy snake should be cast off in a single piece. Mite infestations or an atmosphere that is too dry

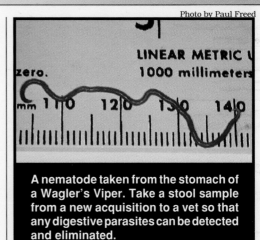

Photo by Paul Freed

A nematode taken from the stomach of a Wagler's Viper. Take a stool sample from a new acquisition to a vet so that any digestive parasites can be detected and eliminated.

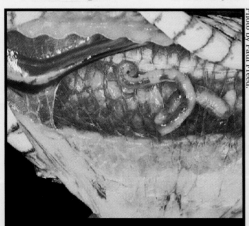

Photo by Paul Freed.

A pentastomid worm in the lung of a Wagler's Viper. This is the typical site of infection by pentastomids, causing secondary bacterial infections and pneumonia.

for the species may result in the skin being shed in fragments. This allows the lubricating fluid between the old and new skin to dry out too quickly, resulting in parts of the old skin staying put. Infection can build up under unshed skin, causing further problems.

A snake having shedding

difficulties should be placed for a half hour or so in a bath of lukewarm water so that the skin can soften. Often the problem skin will fall away in the water, but any remainder can usually be gently peeled off with the fingers.

One particular shedding problem is a failure to shed the old eye spectacle (which is part of the skin). In severe cases a snake may be almost blinded by having several layers of dulled spectacles left from previous sheddings. The spectacle should be lubricated with a little mineral oil over a

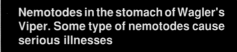

Nemotodes in the stomach of Wagler's Viper. Some type of nemotodes cause serious illnesses

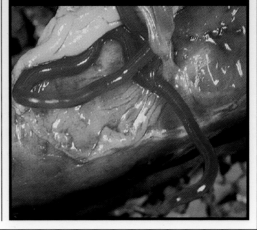

period of two to three days. Once loosened, the spectacle can be gently lifted away with a fingernail, taking great care not to damage the new spectacle beneath. If shedding difficulties are a constant problem in your snakes, you should seriously reconsider the conditions in which you are housing them.

Abscesses

These usually are caused by pathogens entering the skin through a wound, sometimes only a tiny, almost unnoticeable one. The infected area begins to swell and fill with pus, causing an unpleasant looking lump beneath the snake's skin. Large abscesses may have to be surgically opened, drained, and irrigated by a veterinarian before being stitched up. The treatment usually is accompanied with a course of antibiotics.

Ticks and Mites

Ticks are commonly found on wild-caught snakes. These parasites need to feed on blood in order to complete their life cycles. The tick attaches itself to the snake's skin, usually in the softer tissue between a scale or especially near the end of the tail, with its piercing and sucking mouthparts. Once on the snake it will stay there for several days, slowly engorging itself with blood. Newly purchased snakes should be carefully inspected for ticks. The parasites can be easily removed by first dabbing them with a little alcohol to make them relax their grip, and then gently pulling them out with a twisting motion. Large ticks can be removed with your fingers, smaller ones using tweezers. The ticks found on snakes are not known to carry Lyme disease, but a little common sense should tell

A nematode worm infecting the skin of a Plainbelly Watersnake, *Nerodia erythrogaster*. Look at any potential purchase closely and carefully; don't buy a specimen that shows signs of ill-health or parasites.

Photo by Paul Freed.

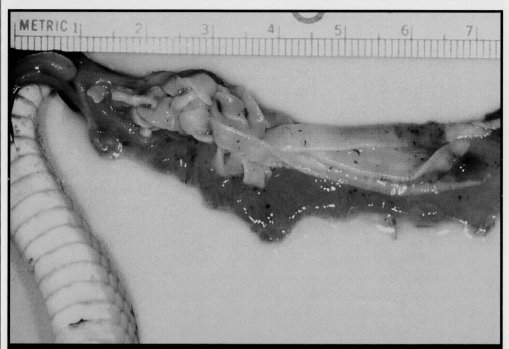

Tapeworms in the stomach of a South American snake, *Liophis poecilogyrus*; these cestodes commonly infect wild-caught snakes.

you not to squish the tick in your fingers; dispose of it by dropping the body into a small bottle of rubbing alcohol.

Mites often are much more of a problem in captive snakes than are ticks. These tiny, pin-head sized parasites tend to occur in large numbers and may infest the whole of the snake quarters as well as the snakes themselves. Mites tend not to stay attached to the snake's body for as long as ticks, but they feed frequently and, in large numbers, can cause severe irritation with accompanying stress and anemia. Both ticks and mites also are capable of transmitting blood pathogens from one reptile to another. Regular thorough cleansing of the snake quarters will help avoid a mite infestation, but if an infestation occurs you must treat it immediately before the parasites breed out of control. Heavy infestations on small snakes can lead to death and also greatly hamper shedding and even reproduction.

Recently, a number of reptile-safe acaricides have appeared on the market. These are much safer than previous chemicals and should be used, according to the manufacturer's recommendations, wherever possible. Your pet shop will be able to advise you on suitable products for routine preventive treatments and minor infestations.

Worm Infections

Wild-caught snakes often are infected with intestinal worms. Under conditions of stress these can multiply to numbers that can be dangerous to the snake's health. It is recommended that you send fecal samples from your snakes to a veterinary laboratory for monitoring. (This must be done through your veterinarian, who may even be able to make simple tests in his office.) Examination of the feces will show the type and seriousness of an infestation. Snakes with worm (helminth) infections should be treated with a vermicide as recommended by your veterinarian. Recently a few general-purpose reptile wormers have appeared on the pet market, but some vets question their safety and effectiveness as well as the ability of hobbyists to properly dose small animals. Most wormers are toxic, so their dosage must be carefully controlled.

Injuries

Most flesh injuries arise as a result of male combat and are especially common in booids where two males are kept together with females. Sound husbandry will help prevent such injuries. Deep flesh wounds should be referred to a veterinarian. In recent times much success has been achieved in the surgical repair of flesh wounds, providing they are treated in time. Another major source of wounds is burns due to a snake being able to get too close to a basking light or staying too long on a faulty heated rock. Deep burns often produce severe scarring and may lead to death. A veterinarian should be consulted for all wounds.

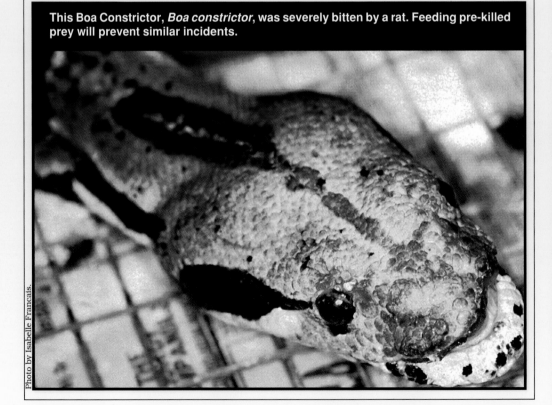

This Boa Constrictor, *Boa constrictor*, was severely bitten by a rat. Feeding pre-killed prey will prevent similar incidents.

Photo by Isabelle Francais.

AN OVERVIEW OF THE SNAKES

With over 3000 species of snakes worldwide, it would be impossible to give a comprehensive list and descriptions in a volume of this size. Instead, we will focus briefly on those snake genera and species that seem to be the most popular and widely available, but still mention a few scarcer and more challenging species to whet the appetites of those who may one day wish to specialize. The vast majority of "pet" snakes are members of the families Boidae, Pythonidae, and Colubridae, and it is these families on which we will concentrate in this book. There are several other families of snakes that have little attraction to hobbyists, such as the blind snakes, Typhlopidae and their relatives, and the shieldtails, Uropeltidae, and they will not be further mentioned. Also, because the venomous snakes, Elapidae and Viperidae, are not suitable for the beginner (both for the dangers involved in their care and because of legal problems with permits, etc., in most areas) they are not covered here.

FAMILIES BOIDAE AND PYTHONIDAE

The booid snakes include the pythons and the boas, groups that have seen considerable taxonomic controversies and changes over the years. As members of this group command a high profile in herpetoculture,

I'll cover them in fair detail and briefly discuss some of the more popular species. At the present time, the following groups are recognized as either full families or subfamilies of Boidae by different herpetologists.

Boidae contains the New World (the Americas)boas , including *Boa, Corallus, Eunectes,* and *Epicrates,* plus the genera *Acrantophis* and *Sanzinia* of Madagascar and the Pacific boas, *Candoia.* The most popular snake from this family is the Boa Constrictor, *Boa constrictor.* This species, with its common name the same as its scientific one, is

Photo by R. D. Bartlett.

Boa Constrictors, *B. constrictor*, are hardy, large, beautiful, and, usually, docile. Still, an adult boa can be up to 10 feet long and so must be treated with respect.

so well known that it barely requires description. Many subspecies of doubtful validity usually are recognized, but unfortunately indiscriminate captive breeding has resulted in a lot of intersubspecific hybrids. If you intend to breed Boa Constrictors and are lucky enough to get a pure subspecies, try to keep the strain pure. Cooperation between hobbyists and careful record-keeping will go a long way toward preserving some subspecies if it is done in time. Boa Constrictors require a large cage with tropical conditions and medium humidity. Juvenile specimens will feed on mice, small rats, or chicks; adults feed on large rats or chickens.

A similar situation exists with the Rainbow Boa, *Epicrates cenchria*, of which there are about a dozen subspecies usually

When buying a baby Rainbow Boa, *E. cenchria*, look at the parents, if you can. Some grow up to be absolutely brilliant red animals, while others are brown or tan.

recognized. As with the Boa Constrictors, I consider it important that pure lines of subspecies be maintained during captive breeding efforts. Growing to a maximum of about 7 ft/2.1 m, Rainbow Boas occur in various shades of brown with lighter and/or darker stripes, spots, and ocelli. Their common name arises from the iridescent sheen of the skin that is particularly beautiful in specimens that have recently shed. Rainbow Boas can be kept in a medium sized cage with tropical temperatures and medium to high humidity conditions and will do well on a staple diet of mice. Other popular members of the genus *Epicrates* that can be kept in similar conditions include the Haitian Boa, *E. striatus*, the

Cuban Boa, *E. angulifer*, and the Puerto Rican Boa, *E. inornatus*.

The Green Anaconda, *Eunectes murinus*, is not generally recommended for the average hobbyist due to its mean disposition and the fact that it can grow to an enormous size (28 ft/8.5 m has been recorded, though most specimens are smaller). It is generally olive-green in color with darker blotches. It requires tropical conditions in an extremely large terrarium with a sizable water bath. Juveniles will feed on rats, fish, chicks, etc., but adults will require large food items such as adult chickens, ducks, or rabbits. If you must have an anaconda, the smaller Yellow Anaconda, *Eunectes notaeus*, is perhaps a better choice.

Although beautiful, Emerald Tree Boas, *C. caninus*, are somewhat difficult to keep. Some keepers suggest using full-spectrum lighting with this species.

The Emerald Tree Boa, *Corallus caninus*, is a colorful and popular species. The maximum length is about 7 ft/2.1 m. Adults are emerald-green with a yellow belly and a series of narrow white bands across the back. Juveniles may be red or yellow. They require humid tropical conditions in a tall terrarium with adequate climbing branches.

Photo by Karl H. Switak

Use a very heavy and stable water bowl in a Burrowing Python, *Calabaria reinhardti*, enclosure, otherwise the snake frequently will tip it.

Calabariidae contains the single monotypic genus *Calabaria*. The West African Burrowing Python, *Calabaria reinhardti*, occasionally turns up in collections. This is an interesting looking snake that grows to about 3 ft 6 in/1.1 m in total length. The color is brown to reddish brown with irregular reddish markings. It requires a moist tropical terrarium with burrowing facilities. As far as I am aware it has not been successfully bred in captivity, though small clutches of relatively large eggs laid by gravid imported females are successfully incubated from time to time.

Erycinidae contains the North

Since the sand boas, like this Rough Sand Boa, *Eryx conicus*, are nicely patterned, stay fairly small, and are easy to keep, their waxing popularity is no surprise.

Photo by Isabelle Francais.

American genera *Charina* (rubber boas) and *Lichanura* (rosy boas) and the Old World (Africa, Europe, Asia) genus *Eryx* (sand boas). Rubber, rosy, and sand boas include several popular terrarium subjects. The Rubber Boa, *Charina bottae*, of western North America, grows to about 27 in/70 cm. It is plain brown to bright olive on the back, lighter beneath. It is a secretive burrowing snake that requires a moist, temperate terrarium with adequate burrowing facilities. Adults feed on mice. The Rosy Boa, *Lichanura trivirgata*, also is from western North America. This is a very attractive species with several subspecies and color varieties, and it is very popular at

Sand boas should be given a substantial temperature reduction at night to simulate their wild environment. This is a Kenyan Sand Boa, *E. colubrinus loveridgei*.

Photo by Isabelle Francais.

the moment in the hobby. Maximum length is about 30 in/ 76 cm. They may be kept in a temperate to warm terrarium and will feed on mice.

Some of the sand boas are fairly popular. They are relatively small and thus can be kept in a small terrarium. The Kenyan Sand Boa, *Eryx colubrinus*, is one of the most popular varieties. This attractive, heavy-bodied snake reaches about 28 in/70 cm in length. The normal variety is chocolate brown to almost black, marked with a series of yellow to orange blotches. The underside is white. They are best kept in a fairly small tank with a deep, sandy substrate. They like to bask in temperatures up to 100°F/38°C, but must have a cooler spot available in the cage. Water should always be available in a small dish. They will feed readily on a diet of mice. Albino and xanthic varieties now are available.

Loxocemidae contains only the Mexican and Central American *Loxocemus bicolor*, the Neotropical Burrowing Python, which grows to about 4 ft/1.2 m in length and is usually iridescent brownish in color with a lighter underside. It requires similar care to *Calabaria*.

Photo by Isabelle Francais.

If you purchase a wild-caught Ball Python, *P. regius*, check it carefully for ticks, as wild individuals frequently have them.

Pythonidae contains the typical Old World pythons, *Python*, and the Australasian pythons of the genera *Antaresia, Aspidites*, and *Liasis*. Of the typical pythons, the Burmese, *P. molurus bivittatus*, and the Ball, *P. regius*, are probably the most widely kept by hobbyists. The Burmese in particular is bred frequently in captivity and is available in several color forms. The major limiting factor of the Burmese is its size; an adult female can reach 20 ft/6 m or more in length! They require a large terrarium with tropical conditions and a large water bath. Juveniles can be raised on mice, graduating to rats, then finally chickens and rabbits as they mature. The attractive African Ball Python, named after its habit of rolling into a ball when scared, can be kept in similar conditions, but as its maximum length is only about 6 ft/1.8 m, smaller accommodations will be satisfactory. Wild-caught juveniles are the cheapest pythons available, but they seldom feed, are highly stressed and diseased, and often die in a few weeks. Captive-bred Ball Pythons, on the other hand, adapt well and are worth the extra money. The Blood Python, *P. curtus*, from Southeast Asia also is making inroads into the hobby and is being successfully bred. They are robust, colorful pythons, growing to an average length of 6 ft/1.8 m. The three subspecies should be kept genetically pure if possible. They require moist tropical conditions with adequate hiding places and will feed on rats or chickens. This species is notorious for its aggressive demeanor when handled.

A very attractive but rare python is Boelen's, *P. boeleni*, from the jungles of New Guinea.

This is a medium sized snake, glossy jet black with a yellow or cream belly that extends into irregular oblique stripes along the flanks. If you are lucky enough to get hold of any specimens, you should take great care of them and make every attempt to breed them. They require moist tropical conditions in the terrarium and can be fed on rats, mice, and chickens.

Some of the Australasian pythons (those of New Guinea and Australia) are gaining in popularity in the hobby. Many of the species formerly were placed in the genus *Morelia*, now often considered a synonym of *Python*. The Carpet Python, *Python*

Photo by Karl H. Switak

Carpet Pythons, *P. spilotus variegatus*, are being bred by more hobbyists, so they should become more affordable soon.

spilotus variegatus and related subspecies or color forms, is probably the best known and most frequently available, while another subspecies, the Diamond Python, *P. spilotus spilotus*, is a herpetologist's "prize" if it can be obtained. The Carpet Python got its common name from the intricate buff, black, and yellow "carpet" pattern of its skin, while the Diamond Python is named for the vaguely diamond-shaped spots on a blackish background. Both subspecies grow to about 10 ft/3 m and can be maintained in a terrarium with medium dry subtropical conditions, though a water bath should always be available. They will feed on mice, rats, and chickens. Australia protects all its reptiles from export, so specimens usually come from western New Guinea (part of Indonesia) or are captive-bred. Carpet Pythons recently have been bred in good numbers representative of several color patterns, though they remain expensive.

Tropidophiidae contains the dwarf and wood boas of Central and South America and the West Indies of the genera *Exiliboa*, *Trachyboa*, *Tropidophis*, and *Ungaliophis*. Most of these small booids, though some would make good tropical terrarium subjects, are rarely available in the hobby. If you are lucky enough to obtain specimens, they should be kept in small terraria with tropical conditions. Though frogs and/or lizards seem to be the preferred food of most species, some success has been achieved in converting captive specimens to a diet of mice.

FAMILY COLUBRIDAE

This is an extremely complex family that is impossible to define scientifically and contains a diverse assortment of very different-looking snakes. Authorities recognize numerous subfamilies of uncertain limits, and genera commonly shift from

Photo by John C. Murphy.

The more advanced hobbyist may want to try caring for the Strange-scaled Snake, *Xenodermus javanicus*, if one can be found. Very little is known about their natural history.

one group to another on a regular basis. Virtually all the species seen in the hobby belong to the subfamilies Colubrinae and Natricinae, the typical snakes and the water snakes. Some of the subfamilies are listed here, with notes on a few of the more popular genera.

Xenoderminae contains the odd-scaled snakes. The subfamily is named after the Oriental *Xenodermus*, in which the various sized dorsal scales are rather uniquely arranged in patterns. Four further genera occur in Southeast Asia and two more in tropical Central and South America. Little is known about the biology of these snakes at the present time, and they rarely turn up in the hobby. It has been suggested that they require humid, tropical conditions in the terrarium. *Xenodermus* is a fairly plain brown snake with a lighter underside. It grows to about 26 in/65 cm in total length and feeds largely on frogs.

Sibynophinae, the many-toothed snakes, consists of three genera, the best known being *Sibynophis* of Southeast Asia. The

Chinese Mountain Snake, *Sibynophis chinensis*, ranges from southern China to Vietnam. It is a small, slender snake, with a maximum length of 24 in/60 cm. It is grayish brown above, sometimes with a darker vertebral stripe, while the underside is whitish with dark spots. The head is black, separated from the brown of the body by a narrow yellowish collar. They can be kept in a relatively small terrarium with subtropical conditions. They will do well in captivity as long as a diet of lizards or a good substitute can be provided.

Photo by Paul Freed.

Some scientists speculate that the hognose snakes, like this Mexican Hognose, *Heterodon nasicus kennerlyi*, have a venom that specifically affects amphibians.

Xenodontinae, odd-toothed snakes, contains approximately 27 genera of snakes confined to the Americas. Some of them are rear-fanged and mildly venomous, but all have some enlarged teeth in the rear of the jaw. The best known genus is probably *Heterodon*, which contains the North American hognose snakes. These snakes have the intriguing habit of "playing dead" when disturbed, turning over onto their back with the mouth hanging open, but if they are uprighted, they immediately turn over onto the back again! The Western Hognose Snake, *Heterodon nasicus*, is a typical example and the one that is probably most suited to captivity. It ranges from southern central Canada to Texas and northern Mexico. The pointed snout is upturned sharply and the head is barely set off from the stout body by the thick neck. The maximum length is 35 in/88 cm. The color is variable through gray, brown, or reddish brown above, with a series of darker blotches along the back and two to three rows of spots along the flanks. The belly is marked with large black patches. A pair of hognose snakes can be kept comfortably in a 20-gallon tank with a coarse sand substrate. Climate should be dry temperate with a basking light. A winter rest period at reduced temperatures may lead to breeding. Wild-caught specimens feed on frogs, toads, and/or lizards, but captive-bred specimens should be adapted to mice, making them easier to keep.

Calamarinae has been called the dwarf snakes. With over 70 species in about ten genera, these small, secretive, mainly burrowing, Southeast Asian snakes range from just 8 in/20 cm to 24 in/60 cm in total length. They are rarely seen as captives and make poor pets, though some are brightly colored.

Colubrinae is the typical or common snakes. This is a large subfamily containing about 50 genera and more than 300 species, many of which are very popular in the hobby. Colubrines are found in many habitats and

Photo by R. D. Bartlett

Eastern Yellowbelly Racers, *Coluber constrictor flaviventris*, and other members of the genus tend to be nervous captives. Provide them with a spacious cage and plenty of hiding places.

include arboreal, terrestrial, burrowing, and semiaquatic species. Some of most popular genera in the hobby include *Coluber*, racers; *Drymarchon*, indigo snakes; *Elaphe*, ratsnakes; and *Lampropeltis*, kingsnakes and milk snakes.

Photo by Isabelle Francais

The Corn Snake, *E. guttata*, was one of the first snakes to be bred on a commercial scale. As a result of this, many "designer" colors and patterns are now available.

The best known racer is the American Racer, *Coluber constrictor*, which occurs over most of the USA and south as far as Guatemala. Numerous subspecies are usually recognized; all are long (to 6 ft/ 180 cm), slender, fast-moving snakes. The northeastern subspecies, *C. c. constrictor* (the

Ratsnakes climb frequently, so give them branches in the terrarium. This is the Everglades Ratsnakes, *E. obsoleta rossalleni.*

Northern Black Racer), is more or less uniformly slate black, but other subspecies vary in color from brown through yellowish, greenish, or bluish; juveniles have a strong pattern of brown bands across the back. Most can be kept in a medium sized terrarium with temperate conditions and dry to medium humidity. Feed on mice or chicks. European racers in the genus *Coluber* (sometimes regarded as *Hierophis*) include the Horseshoe Snake, *C. hippocrepis,* and the Caspian Whipsnake, *C. jugularis.* These can be kept in similar conditions to North American racers.

The Indigo Snake, *Drymarchon corais,* occurs in several

California Kingsnakes, *L. g. californiae,* are probably the most frequently bred subspecies of kingsnake; it is frequently available.

subspecies from the southeastern USA to Argentina. The most popular subspecies is the Eastern Indigo Snake, *D. c. couperi,* which occurs in Florida and southern Georgia and adjacent states. This is the largest North American snake and can reach over 8 ft/2.4 m in length. The Eastern Indigo is glossy blue-black with a yellow to orange chin and facial spotting. This Indigo Snake is strictly protected in the wild. There are a number of captive breeding programs underway, but currently the subspecies is not

Kingsnakes should always be housed separately, as they frequently eat snakes and lizards in the wild. This is a striped-phase Blotched Kingsnake, *L. g. floridana* "goini.

available to the average hobbyist. Subspecies from Mexico and South America occasionally are available, however. They can be kept in conditions similar to *Coluber.*

The ratsnakes, *Elaphe,* include some of the most popular of terrarium subjects. They are being bred extensively for the pet market and many species come in a number of exciting color mutations. The beloved Cornsnake, *E. guttata,* of the eastern USA, in its natural form is one of the most attractive snakes, with its pinkish body marked with a series of dark-bordered red blotches. Several color varieties are available. Growing to a maximum of 6 ft/180 cm, Cornsnakes become very docile pets. They can be kept in a dry to medium-moist terrarium in temperate conditions. They will feed readily on mice. The ratsnakes of the *Elaphe obsoleta* complex also are very popular in the hobby and can be kept in similar conditions, as can some of the European ratsnakes, such as the Aesculapean Snake, *E.*

The subspecies of the milk snake are highly variable and difficult to identify. This Costa Rican specimen could be any of three subspecies: Black, Honduran, or Stuart's.

The Desert Kingsnake, *L. g. splendida*, is not as commonly kept as many of the other kingsnake subspecies.

longissima; the Four-lined Snake, *E. quatuorlineata*; and the Leopard Snake, *E. situla*.

The American kingsnakes and milk snakes of the genus *Lampropeltis* form one of the most complex groups of commonly kept terrarium subjects. Their captive docility, spectacular coloration, and ease with which they adapt to mice, chicks, and young rats as a staple diet make many of the species and subspecies extremely popular. The most commonly kept species is the Common Kingsnake, *Lampropeltis getula*, which occurs in several

subspecies and color mutations. Other species include the highly complex and colorful milk snakes or tricolored kingsnakes, such as *L. triangulum*, *L. pyromelana*, and *L. zonata*. All can be kept in medium sized cages in subtropical to temperate conditions depending on where they originated.

Dasypeltinae contains a few species of African egg-eating snakes. Though not frequently available, the African egg-eaters are extremely interesting and are relatively easy to keep. They should be kept in tropical conditions in a small terrarium,

The Sinaloan Milk Snake, *L. t. sinaloae*, is one of the most frequently bred subspecies of milk snake. This individual has a broken pattern.

The Pine Snake, *Pituophis melanoleucus*, and its relatives can be kept in conditions similar to kingsnakes. Pine Snakes tend to get larger, and some have nasty temperaments.

generally under relatively dry conditions. Small specimens should be fed on quail or pigeon eggs, while larger specimens can take bantam or full size chicken eggs.

Lycodontinae, the wolf snakes, were named for their large, fanglike teeth. Perhaps the best known member of the subfamily is the African House Snake, *Boaedon fuliginosus*, which occurs over the southern half of Africa. Growing to about 3 ft/90 cm in length, this is a plain brown snake, lighter beneath, with a distinctive light stripe on either side of the snout. This species is a relatively easy captive. It should

The African House Snake, *Boaedon fulginosus*, is a pretty and hardy snake that, unfortunately, is seldom available.

be kept in medium dry conditions and will do well on a diet of mice.

Natricinae includes the water snakes and their allies. Many of these should only be loosely regarded as semiaquatic snakes, being quite terrestrial, though nearly all of them like moist conditions. There are about 40 genera, of the which the most popular is perhaps the North American *Thamnophis*, the garter snakes. The Common Garter Snake, *T. sirtalis*, with several subspecies, is best known as a "beginner's snake" as it is so easy

Because it is mildly venomous and often aggressive, the Chinese Paddy Snake, *Enhydris chinensis*, is not recommended for beginners. This specimen has an aberrant pale color.

to keep, feeding on a diet of earthworms and small freshwater fishes. Several other species in the genus *Thamnophis* also are easy pets.

Typical North American water snakes of the genus *Nerodia* include several species highly suited to terrarium life. Most of these will feed on a diet of fishes. The best known species is probably the Northern Water Snake, *N. sipedon*. It requires an aquaterrarium with temperate conditions and with dry basking facilities. (If kept too moist and not allowed to dry, skin blisters will develop and could lead to death.) European grass snakes of the genus *Natrix* can be kept in a similar manner but need even less water.

Homalopsinae contains the rear-fanged water snakes. Included among its eight genera is *Enhydris*, a group of snakes from Southeast Asia. The Chinese Paddy Snake, *E. chinensis*, is one of the better known species. It bears a superficial resemblance to some species of *Nerodia* and may be kept in similar conditions. The venom from the bite of this rather

The Boomslang, *Dispholidus typus*, is one of the few dangerously venomous colubrids. Venomous snakes must be kept in securely locked enclosures at all times.

Photo by Mark Smith.

Garter snakes will thrive in captivity if fed a wide variety of foods: earthworms, insects, live fish, and pinky mice. This is the Checkered Garter Snake, *Thamnophis marcianus.*

Photo by Isabelle Francais.

snappy snake is not known to be fatal to humans, but it has caused headaches, pain, and nausea, so it should be treated with respect.

Boiginae is an artificial group of rear-fanged snakes. With over 70 genera this is the largest of the colubrid subfamilies. In most species the venom is not dangerous to humans, but, to be on the safe side, all should be treated with respect. The Boomslang, *Dispholidus typus*, and the African Bird Snake,

Thelotornis kirtlandi, both of southern Africa, have been responsible for several human fatalities, including the deaths of at least two famous herpetologists! These species are definitely not recommended for beginners. One of the most popular members of the subfamily is the Mangrove Snake, *Boiga dendrophila*, which, with its glossy black scales and vivid yellow markings, is a very attractive species. Though it has a fairly nasty disposition, as far as I know its bite is not particularly dangerous though I would be very careful with it—there are persistent rumors of it having

Although not believed to be dangerously venomous, *Boiga drapiezi* and the other mangrove snakes are best treated like venomous specimens.

Photo by W. Wüster.

caused human deaths. It grows to about 6 ft/180 cm in length and seems to prefer chicks over mice, but will eat the latter if no chicks are available. It requires a tall, humid, tropical terrarium with adequate climbing branches.

Dipsadinae, the South American snail-eating snakes,

whether they are actually related. Similar remarks can be made about their habits and care.

Elachistodontinae contains only the Indian Egg-eating Snake, *Elachistodon westermanni*, a rare snake from northern India and vicinity of which little seems to be known.

Photo by R. D. Bartlett.

The Rough-scaled Bush Viper, *Atheris squamiger*, is a beautiful but dangerous animal. Only the most experienced hobbyist should consider keeping these snakes.

includes three genera. This interesting group has developed a means of removing snails, their main diet, from their shells. Not widely kept as captives, they probably would constitute a challenge to the more serious hobbyist.

Pareinae is the Asian snail-eating snakes. Sometimes included among the Dipsadinae, it is disputed as to whether this is a case of parallel evolution or

Aparallactinae, the false vipers, includes eight genera of African snakes with rear fangs set relatively far forward. Members of the genus *Aparallactus* are commonly known as centipede eaters. The Cape Centipede Eater, *A capensis*, is a small yellowish to brownish snake reaching a maximum of 16 in/40 cm in length; it is capable of overpowering and eating centipedes as large as 6 in/15 cm in length.